TO BE A PILGRIM

TO BE A PILGRIM

The Story of John Bunyan

by

JOYCE REASON

LUTTERWORTH PRESS
GUILDFORD AND LONDON

First paperback edition 1980

ISBN 0 7188 2491 1

PRINTED PHOTOLITHO IN GREAT BRITAIN
BY EBENEZER BAYLIS AND SON, LTD.
THE TRINITY PRESS, WORCESTER, AND LONDON

CONTENTS

I

"ONE HERE WILL CONSTANT BE COME WIND, COME WEATHER!"

IT was dark and chilly on a November evening, three hundred years ago—November 12, 1660, to be exact. Little groups of men and women, wrapped in their dark cloaks, could scarcely see the path as they made their way under the bare elm trees to a lonely Bedfordshire farmhouse. They carried no lanterns, as country people usually did at night; and when one party almost ran up against another at the entrance to the farm (a small drawbridge over a moat), they started, and whispered nervously, "Who goes there?" and were only reassured when the others answered cautiously, "Friends."

The big farmhouse kitchen, which had been cleared and set with benches for the meeting, was warm and cheerful in the light of a bright fire and several tallow candles, but the windows were all closely shuttered. As the company sat down and loosened their cloaks, it could be seen that they were most of them poorly dressed, with work-hardened hands and weather-beaten faces. You would guess that they were farm labourers and small tradesmen—tailors, cobblers and such like, with one or two better-off shopkeepers. All of them looked worried and anxious, glancing over their shoulders at every sound, and talking together in low tones. The farmer, master of the house, fidgeted to and fro.

They were waiting for someone, and they were afraid.

*　　*　　*

Here he was at last! A firm step on the flagged courtyard, a single knock at the heavy door. Quickly the farmer drew back the bolts and let in a tall, broad-shouldered figure, ruddy haired, with bright grey eyes and a mouth which curled up at the corners.

"Peace to this house!" said the newcomer in a strong voice. "Peace to you, brothers and sisters."

"Brother Bunyan!" The farmer clutched the rough homespun sleeve. "Brother Bunyan, we have had bad news. We think—we think perhaps you should not preach to-night."

"Ay? What have you heard?" Bunyan did not appear at all surprised or upset. He guessed what was coming.

"Brother, we have certain news that Mr. Francis Wingate—the Justice of the Peace, you know— has put out a warrant for your arrest, and means to send the constable to take you this very night.

He has found out where we are meeting. Now I can tell you that Mr. Wingate is very hot against us, and has sworn to break up our meetings, and if he arrests you he will send you to prison for sure. So would it not be better for you to get away quietly while you can?"

There was a little stir among the waiting people. What would their leader choose to do?

Bunyan spoke out cheerfully. "By no means! I will not stir, nor will I have the meeting put off for this. Come, be of good cheer; our cause is good, we need not be ashamed to preach God's word."

"It is you we are afraid for, Brother Bunyan," said the farmer.

"Nothing can happen to me unless my Lord allows it," Bunyan answered. "Well! It is not quite time for our meeting, and there may be other brothers and sisters on the way. I will just step out into the courtyard for a little, while we are waiting."

He went out again into the dark, and they heard his steps falling steadily, up and down, up and down, and they wondered what he was thinking. He was, indeed, considering seriously whether he was doing right in staying to preach in spite of the warning.

"Well," his thoughts went, "I have always shown myself hearty and courageous in my preaching, and, thank God, I have been able to encourage others; so if I now run away and make an escape, it will look very bad. What will my weak and newly converted brethren think of it? That I was not so strong in deed, as I was in word. And then, if I run now, perhaps when their turn comes to face arrest—and come it will, I am sure of that—they may be afraid and discouraged. And besides, what will the outsiders, and those that wish us ill, say? That John Bunyan the bold preacher was a coward when it came to the point, and did not really believe all the brave things he had been saying about trusting in the Lord. They will think that is what all these Dissenters are like. I will not go."

So back he went into the kitchen of the farm.

"Brothers and sisters, let us pray!"

Prayer over, a few shabby Bibles were brought out. By no means all the congregation could read, and of those that could, some had to follow the words painfully with a gnarled finger. But the Gospels were so well known to them that they could have recited nearly every word without a book.

Then it came, the sound they had all been expecting; the heavy tramp of feet and a thundering blow on the door.

"Open, in the king's name!"

*   *   *

"It's the constable!" the whisper went round.

"Open, brother," said Bunyan quietly, and the farmer drew back the bolts again. Two men, the country constable and a servant of Mr. Justice Wingate, pushed into the quiet room.

"John Bunyan, tinker?"

"I am John Bunyan."

"I've a warrant here for your arrest, for unlawfully preaching and assembling the people together. You're to go before Mr. Wingate—come along with you, quick now!"

"I'm coming," answered Bunyan calmly; then he turned to his people. "Well, you see we are prevented for this time from hearing the Word of God, and it seems that we shall have to suffer for it. But keep up your hearts! It is better to suffer in a good cause, than as thieves or murderers or for any other wickedness. Better to be the persecuted than the persecutors——"

"Oh leave off your canting and come along!" exclaimed the constable.

The two men gripped Bunyan by the arms, though he made no struggle, and hustled him outside. Two or three of the bolder spirits among the congregation got up and followed. They found the constable and Mr. Wingate's man having an argument; for it appeared that, having arrested their man according to orders, they did not know what to do with him.

"I tell you," Wingate's servant was saying,

"it's no manner of use bringing him up to Mr. Wingate's house to-night. His worship's away from home."

"Then where be I to put him?" The constable scratched his· head. "If I lock him up, I'll have to set a watch on him."

"Clap him in the gaol," advised the servant.

"Can't do that without a *mittimus*," said the constable, "and as you know very well, only Mr. Wingate can write out a *mittimus*."

"Well, then, lock him up and watch him your-self!"

"Nay, I've got my other duties," argued the constable, who had no idea of losing his night's rest over the prisoner. "Some'un 'd have to be paid to watch him, and who's to be chargeable for that?"

The prisoner's hearty laugh rang out. "What, am I such a dangerous fellow?" he asked.

One of his friends, who was a fairly well-to-do tradesman from Bedford town, stepped forward. "Bring him to my house, constable," he suggested. "I'll be answerable for him, and bring him to you in the morning. Then you can take him to Mr. Wingate when his worship returns."

"Ah, but how do I know as you won't let him 'scape?"

"I could have escaped any time in the last hour, had I been so minded," said Bunyan. "I promise you I'll keep my appointment with Mr. Wingate."

"And I'll answer for him," added his friend.

"Well"—the constable sounded relieved—"if so be as you'll swear to deliver the prisoner——"

"Friend, I do not swear. But I solemnly promise."

"I'll take your word then." And so the "dangerous" prisoner was given into the hands of his friends, and Bunyan spent his last comfortable night for many a long year.

2

A SLICE OF HISTORY

YOU can go to any church you like. You can be a Roman Catholic, an Anglican, a Congregationalist, Baptist, Methodist, Quaker or a member of any other of the Christian Churches. You can be a Muslim if you want to, or a Hindu or Buddhist or nothing at all, and the law of Britain will not interfere with you as long as *you* do not interfere with other people. You do not have to meet in secret, wondering if at any minute soldiers will break in on you and drag you off to prison, or if you will be taken before a judge and fined so much that you have practically nothing left to live on.

It was not always like that. There was a time when those in power thought that everyone in the Kingdom must worship in the same way. First the Roman Church was supreme. Then, when King Henry VIII quarrelled with the Pope and made himself Head of the Church, it was the Anglican way. When his daughter Mary came to the throne the Roman Catholics were in power again, and under Elizabeth I, James I and Charles I it was the Anglicans once more. The only ministers who were supposed to hold services were priests ordained by a bishop, and they had to use the forms set out in the Book of Common Prayer.

These prayers are very beautiful, and many people get great help from them and find in the Church of England all that they need to worship God. But there have always been some who felt that they could not pray properly in a set form of words, and who did not see why, if a man had a gift for preaching and the Word of God was in him, he should not be allowed to preach even if he had not been ordained by a bishop. They also thought that there was no need for the special robes and vestments worn by the priests, and that the Church of England services were very different from the meetings of the Church in the early days of the Apostles. Because they wanted what they felt was a "purer" kind of worship, they came to be called Puritans. There were Puritans within the Church of England, as well as those who became Presbyterians, Independents (Congregationalists), Baptists, and Quakers.

*   *   *

In the days of Elizabeth, James and Charles, the Dissenters (to put them all together under one heading) had a rather bad time. They were fined, imprisoned and persecuted so much that, in the reign of James I, many of them decided to go off to America and settle there. These were the Pilgrim Fathers, who were some of the founders of the United States of America. We are concerned with those who remained behind and struggled on. They were not the only ones who were persecuted; the Roman Catholics had a bad time too.

In the reign of King Charles I the king and Parliament quarrelled, and finally war broke out between the two sides—a dreadful thing to happen to a country. The Parliamentary side won, and King Charles was executed. So for a while there was no king, but what was known as a Commonwealth; and the greatest man in the Commonwealth was Oliver Cromwell, the famous general, who was made Lord Protector. Cromwell himself was an Independent, that is, a Congregationalist, and so was most of his army, so now it was the Dissenters who had the power, and the Roman Catholics and Anglicans who suffered.

For that was the sad thing—every group of Christians, as soon as they came to power, started to suppress and persecute the others. The Prayer Book was forbidden, and many Anglican priests had to leave their churches. But it must be said that Oliver Cromwell was not a persecutor, and as long as men did not try to overthrow the

Commonwealth or make a nuisance of themselves, they were not imprisoned or tormented. On the whole, while Cromwell was ruler there was more freedom of worship than there had ever been.

* * *

But Cromwell died, and there was no one who could take his place. So King Charles II, son of the first Charles, was invited back. On a windy May morning in 1660, with the bells ringing and the flags flying and people cheering themselves wild, the tall dark young king landed at Dover and made his way to London and his crowning. And for the Dissenters everything was changed.

Charles II, lazy and easy-going, as well as shrewd and clever, would willingly have left everyone to worship in their own way as long as they acknowledged him as king. Indeed, he had promised to do so before he became king. But his friends and supporters wanted to be revenged on the Dissenters, and being by far the largest party in the new Parliament, they lost no time in bringing in laws against the conventicles, as they called the Dissenters' meetings, and insisting that all services should be conducted according to the Church of England. Actually, these laws did not pass until the following year, but there were plenty of magistrates with a grudge against the Puritans who were ready to go ahead of the law! Which brings us to that dark November evening when the tinker-preacher, John Bunyan, was arrested at the moated farmhouse for preaching the Word of God without a licence.

3

"AWAY WITH SUCH A FELLOW!"

MR. Francis Wingate, red-faced, obstinate and haughty, sat behind a table in his hall **at** Harlington House. His short jacket showed the fine frilled sleeves of his shirt and his wide breeches were adorned with knots of ribbon. A velvet cloak and plumed hat lay carelessly over a carved chair. He made a fine contrast to the heavily booted figure in rough brown homespun who stood before him. Though he was only a boy at the time of the Civil War—he was about the same age as Bunyan—his family, being Royalist, had had to pay a fairly heavy fine when the Parliamentary party came to power. Still, he had not fared so badly, for he had been able to keep Harlington Hall. For all that, he meant, now that the tables were turned, to get his own back on anyone of the opposite side who fell into his clutches.

"So! You caught the rascals at their conventicle!" he addressed the constable. "Well done. And what were the rogues doing when you got there?" He hoped the constable would say that they had weapons with them.

"Well, sir"—the constable looked puzzled—"there was only a few on them, as was met together to hear the preaching, and I didn't see no sign of naught else."

"You fool!" Wingate's face grew even redder. He started to say something more, then thought better of it. He knew he was on shaky ground, as no law had yet been passed against· private preaching, though there had been an order that the Prayer Book was to be used in all churches. But the moated farm was not a church! However, there was an old law from the reign of Queen Elizabeth that might be used. He had got a prisoner, and he was going to make the most of him.

"And what were you doing?" he barked at Bunyan.

"Why," Bunyan answered, "I went to that place, and to other places, to teach the people, to get them to leave their sins, and to come to Christ."

"Aren't you a tinker? Why don't you attend to your business?"

"I think," said Bunyan modestly, "that I can follow my business of tinkering, and preach the Word as well, without confusing the two."

"It's against the law, for people like you to go about preaching."

To which Bunyan returned no answer, for, there being no daily newspapers in those days, he could not be sure whether the law against unlicensed preachers had been passed or not. His silence did not appease Mr. Wingate, however, for his neck swelled and his eyes started out with fury.

"I tell you, I'll break the neck of your meetings!" he choked.

"That may very well be so!" admitted Bunyan with a wry smile.

"You'll go before the judges at the next Session, when they come to Bedford," Wingate went on. "And unless you can get someone to stand surety for you, to gaol you go this very day."

However, two of Bunyan's friends were all ready to stand surety for him, to promise that unless he appeared before the judges they, the friends, would pay a heavy fine. Wingate scowled at them.

"So! You're prepared to give your bond on behalf of a canting tinker!" he sneered. "Very well; but you must promise to keep him from preaching."

Bunyan started forward. "In that case," he said hastily, "I can't accept my friends' offer; for I can't leave off speaking the Word of God. And I should not have thought there was any harm in that, but rather that it was a good thing to do."

"Have it your own way!" Wingate was rather

pleased than otherwise. "If you won't give an undertaking not to preach, I'll make out your *mittimus* and send you to gaol until the Quarter Sessions, when the King's Judges come."

*   *   *

Wingate went off to make out the *mittimus*, the order for Bunyan's imprisonment. No sooner had he gone, than in came the vicar of the neighbouring church. Now seeing that this Dr. Lindale had not been turned out of his church during the Commonwealth, but had been left in peace, one would have thought he would have been more tolerant; but he seems to have had a special spite against Bunyan—perhaps he was jealous of his influence! In any case, he began abusing him, calling him a rogue, and a vagabond and a hypocrite, and a rebel.

At last Bunyan protested wearily, "I didn't come here to talk to you, but to Mr. Justice Wingate."

"Ha! So you've nothing to say for yourself, you ignorant clodhopper!"

"I'm ready to answer any sensible question that's put to me," said Bunyan.

"All right! I ask you, then, how can you prove that it is lawful for you, a common labouring man, to preach?"

"I can prove it to you out of the Bible," Bunyan

answered. "St. Peter says, 'As every man hath received the gift, so let him minister the same.'"

"Ay, and to whom was that spoken?" demanded Dr. Lindale.

"Why, to every one that has received a gift from God. And then again it is said, 'You may all prophesy one by one.'"

Dr. Lindale was somewhat taken aback at this, and could not at once think of an answer. Presently he came back with, "I seem to remember reading about a man called Alexander the Coppersmith, who greatly disturbed the Apostles." That was a dig at Bunyan the tinker.

By this time Bunyan was getting angry—not for nothing did he have red hair—and he replied sharply, "I also have read of many scribes and pharisees, that had their hands in the blood of Christ!"

"Pharisee yourself!" retorted Lindale, "that make long prayers and devour widows' houses!"

Bunyan's temper died down and he could not help laughing. "Ah, Dr. Lindale," he said humorously, "if you had got no more by preaching and praying than I have done, you wouldn't be so rich as you are now!"

All at once it seemed as though words from the Bible sounded in his mind: "Answer not a fool according to his folly!" and he realized that this sort of wrangling was not going to do any good to anyone. So he shut his lips on some

other telling things he might have said. It was
quite a relief when Wingate came back with the
mittimus made out, and the constable and his
prisoner left the Hall to go to Bedford gaol.

*   *   *

They had hardly stepped outside the great
gates, however, when two figures emerged out
of the gloom (for by now the short November day
had closed in). "Wait a minute, constable!"
one of them called. Bunyan recognized the voice
of yet another of his friends.

"What is it now?" the constable growled.
He was tired of this troublesome prisoner and his
friends, and wanted to be free to drink a can of
ale!

"We have been consulting what is the best
to do for you," Bunyan's friends told him. "We
believe we could make Justice Wingate listen to us.
Just wait while we go in and see him."

Bunyan did not think it likely that Wingate
would change his mind, but he did not like to
discourage his loving friends; so he and the constable stood there in the chill and muddy night,
until the two friends came bustling out again.

"It's like this," they told Bunyan, "Mr. Wingate says that if you will come back and say certain
words to him, you will be released."

"If what he wants me to say agrees with my

conscience," said Bunyan, "I am quite willing to say them; but if not, I will not." He did not really expect that he would be let off without making some promise that he could not, in good faith, agree to.

"O God," the weary, anxious prisoner prayed within himself as they trudged up to the Hall once more, "grant me light and strength, that I may not say or do anything wrong!"

*　　*　　*

He was not to be allowed to get it over quickly. As he came into the gloomy hall, where a few tall candles made a little pool of light on the Justice's table, out of another room came Mr. Wingate's brother-in-law, Mr. Foster, holding a candle above his head so that its light fell on the prisoner's face.

"What, John Bunyan!" he exclaimed, coming forward with an oily smile and his free hand outstretched, so that for a moment Bunyan really thought he was going to fling his arm round his neck and kiss him. "How do you do?"

"Why, I hardly know the man!" thought Bunyan, drawing back a little. "He has always been so set against my people—why does he seem so loving all of a sudden? There's something underhand here." Aloud he said, coolly but politely, "I am very well, thank God."

"And what has brought you here?" continued Foster, still with his pleasant manner.

"Why," answered Bunyan, "I was at a meeting of people a little way off, intending to speak to them of God. The Justice, hearing of this, was pleased to send a warrant to fetch me before him."

"So I understood," said Foster. Bunyan thought, "Then why ask me?" but he said nothing. "Now see here," Foster went on coaxingly, "all you have to do is to promise not to call the people together, and you shall be free to go home. My brother-in-law does not want to send you to prison, you know."

Bunyan saw the trap. "Sir," he said, "pray what do you mean by calling the people together?"

"Now, now, you mustn't quibble," said Foster. "Just say that you will not call the people together, and you are free. Otherwise, you must go to prison."

"Sir, I shall not *force* the people to come and listen to me," answered Bunyan with a smile. "But suppose I come where the people are met together, and they want me to speak, I should plead with them to come to the Lord Jesus Christ."

"Come, that sort of thing is not your work. You stick to your tinkering, and you shall have the Justice's favour."

"He means that I shall have Mr. Wingate's pots and kettles to mend," thought Bunyan. "Now he's trying to bribe me." Aloud he said, "As I said to Mr. Wingate, I can mind my own business and the Lord's business too; and I shall do my duty whenever I have the chance."

"But"—Mr. Foster still spoke gently—"your preaching is against the law. I want you to assure me that you will leave off, and not call the people together any more."

Bunyan was ready to drop with weariness, but he answered firmly, "Sir, I cannot make any more promises. I am sure that it is my duty to do the best I can, not only in my trade, but in sharing with others what I have learned of God."

Mr. Foster snorted. "How can an ignorant man like you, that doesn't know any Greek, understand the Scriptures?"

" 'He hath hid His things from the wise and prudent, and revealed them unto babes'," quoted Bunyan.

"No one comes to hear you but a company of foolish, ignorant people!" Foster was losing his temper.

"The foolish and the ignorant have most need of teaching," Bunyan retorted.

*   *   *

Mr. Foster, defeated, flounced out of the hall; but Bunyan was not to be left in peace. One of the Justice's clerks stepped forward.

"Look, John Bunyan," he said smoothly, "you are making things hard for my master, who really wants to let you go free. You have only to say these words, 'I promise not to call the people together again,' and you may go home."

Home! Where his wife and children must be so anxious about him—little blind Mary, his daughter, perhaps, standing by the door and listening for Father's footstep! But though his heart ached, Bunyan was not to be caught.

"There are more ways than one," he said forthrightly, "in which a man might be said to call the people together. For instance, if a man stands up in the market place, and reads aloud from a book, let us say, though he does not actually say to the people, 'Sirs, come here and listen', yet they will come, because they want to hear what he reads. So it might be said that he is calling them together. In the same way, people might come to hear me preach, without my having called them. So you see, I cannot promise not to call people together; for it would be all too easy to accuse me later of breaking my promise."

That was Bunyan's final word, and though both Mr. Wingate and Mr. Foster now came back, and badgered the exhausted man a little longer, at last (probably they wanted their supper!) they gave up, and once more handed him over to the constable to take him to gaol.

As they tramped the pitch-dark lanes into

Bedford, Bunyan was silently praising God for having kept him true and given him strength to hold fast. He was not afraid—he was not even anxious. He simply handed over the care of himself and his loved ones to a loving Father, "and," as he wrote a little later, "went away to prison with God's comfort in my poor soul."

4

"MY NAME AT THE FIRST
WAS GRACELESS"

NO one who knew John Bunyan in his twenties
could have guessed that he would ever
be arrested for preaching! It would not have
surprised them if he had been set in the stocks
for swearing, or hauled up before the justice
of the peace for rowdy behaviour, for if ever there
was a roistering, riotous, blasphemous young
ruffian it was the red-headed son of the tinker
of Elstow, a village just north of Bedford. And
this was in the days of the Commonwealth,
when the Puritans were top-dogs and frowned
solemnly on frivolous behaviour! The magistrates
of Bedford must have been an easy-going lot.

Not that Bunyan was what we should consider
wicked. He was honest, he was no drunkard,
he did not play about with the girls. In fact, he had
married very young, and he dearly loved his girl-
wife and their two babies. He was a good worker,
too, and though they were very poor he managed
by his mending of pots and pans to make a home
for his little family. He and his wife had nothing
at all when they married—"not a dish or a spoon

between us" as he himself said, and they had to live
with his father and stepmother; but by hard work
he did contrive to get a tiny cottage to themselves.
But in his leisure hours he cared only to be off
with the other young fellows, dancing and playing
games on the village green or racketing about the
streets of Bedford. And as his only holiday was on
Sunday, that was the day on which the young
tinker was at his rowdiest.

But his really serious fault, and one which he
came to repent of bitterly, was his continual
swearing. He could not speak two words without
an oath! Yet as a boy of sixteen he had served in the
Parliamentary army, where swearing was strictly
forbidden and the soldiers used to hold prayer
meetings round the camp fire. Perhaps, boylike,
he got bored with the preaching and praying!

*   *   *

It was a strange thing that brought him up
short and cured him of swearing. It happened one
day that he and some other youngsters were
chaffing and drinking together, and Bunyan as
usual was ranting in his loud, foul-mouthed way,
taking the Name of God and Christ in vain; when
one of the women with them—known for a bad lot
and no better than she should be—suddenly
broke out:

"John Bunyan! John Bunyan! You make me

tremble to hear you! I wonder God doesn't strike you dead! You are the worst young fellow in town, and you make all the others as bad as yourself."

Now if this had come from the lips of a parson or a "godly" person, Bunyan would merely have shrugged his shoulders, laughed, and poured out a stream of even worse profanity. But if his language shocked even this bad woman, it must be frightful indeed. He was struck dumb with astonishment; and, strange as it may seem, he never swore again.

There were two selves in John Bunyan at this time. One, that his neighbours saw, was the reckless, rollicking, thoughtless lad who didn't give a hoot for goodness or for religion. The other self, which he kept hidden, was frightened, tormented and wretched, suffering from bad dreams and moods of fearful gloom. His gentle little wife was the only one who knew anything of this secret self, and for her sake he tried to hide it.

The truth was, Bunyan was fighting God. He did not think of God as the loving Father, who "so loved the world that He gave His only-begotten Son", but as a terrible Judge who would send him to hell if he did not please Him. Hell was very real to John Bunyan. Even as a small boy he would wake up, drenched in sweat, from a nightmare of everlasting fire, and would stuff the blanket into his mouth to keep himself from screaming. As he grew older, the horror would come upon him even in the midst of his fun and games, but he would shake it off and plunge into wilder ways in order to forget. Only at night, lying awake and listening to the quiet breathing of his wife and babies, there was no escape from his thoughts.

*   *   *

After the shock of the woman's reproof for his swearing, he began to make an effort to reform. Here his wife could help him.

"Talk to me!" he would beg in the long winter evenings. "Tell me about your good father. I wish I had known him! He would have helped me to be a better man."

For the little wife—we do not even know what her name was—had been an orphan when he married her. Her father, though very poor, was a God-fearing man, and when he died all he left her was two books. One of them was called *The Plain Man's Pathway to Heaven* and the other was *The Practice of Piety*. These books she and her husband would sometimes read together by the light of the fire or a tallow candle, spelling out the words slowly, for neither of them had had much education. To tell the truth, both the books were rather dull, but parts of them pleased Bunyan and set him thinking. One thing at least the books did for him—they gave him practice in reading, so that in the end he could read easily and freely, and also put his thoughts down in writing; though to the end of his days his spelling was shocking, even for those times.

The good people of Elstow were now mightily surprised to see the "swearing tinker" appear a reformed character, going regularly to church, behaving soberly and talking piously. He also read his Bible regularly, over and over again, until he nearly knew it all by heart. Yet, if anything, he was inwardly more miserable than ever.

He was trying hard to please God, not because he loved God, but because he wanted to escape hell! He was being good by rule—and, of course, he found himself continually breaking the rule, if not in deed, then in thought. Whenever he felt most satisfied with himself, bad thoughts would come into his mind, just as if they had been whispered there by Satan. Above all, when he remembered his swearing, and how he had used the holy Name of God, he wondered if he had committed the unforgivable sin. He gave up all the things that pleased him, his games and his dancing, and thought that this, at least, would please God. One thing he loved above all, and found very hard to give up. He was very fond of music, and loved to join in ringing the church bells. One would not think there was anything wrong in that! But poor

Bunyan had got into such a state of mind that he thought anything he really liked must be wicked. He fancied that the bells might come down on his head, or the tower might fall on him, and then he would die, and go straight to hell. Poor young man! It may seem foolish to us, but God was working in his heart all the time, making use even of his foolishness to bring him to Himself.

*　　*　　*

One day, as often happened, his business took him into Bedford town. A pretty little town it was then, with gardens and orchards in the midst of the houses, and the river Ouse flowing soft and clean under its stone bridge. The steeply gabled houses were mostly of lath and plaster, with thatched roofs, and standing up above them one would see the spires of several churches—St. Paul's in the centre, St. Peter's, St. Cuthbert's, and beyond the river to the south, St. John's. It was the church of St. John, furthest from Elstow, that was to make such a change in Bunyan's life, for here he met his Evangelist, who pointed out to him his way to the Celestial City.

So, on this sunny afternoon, we see young Bunyan, his bag of tools on his back, passing through a street of humble cottages. The good wives, their cleaning done, sat spinning at their doors, enjoying the warmth and a good gossip. As he neared one little group, Bunyan heard the Name of God, and slackened his pace to listen. Two or three poor women were talking, not about their homes or their neighbours, but about religion.

"Ha!" thought Bunyan, "I can talk about religion too. I'll stay and join in the talk." For he rather fancied himself as a talker at this time. But as he heard more plainly what they were saying, he found that it was far above his understanding. Not that they were clever women or well educated; very likely they could not read. But they spoke of the love of God, of what Christ had done for them, as if joy overflowed their hearts. They seemed to know the Lord Jesus as a Friend. It seemed to Bunyan that they sat on the sunny side of a mountain, bathed in light and warmth, while he stood shivering on the shadow side in the dark and cold. He knew that he had not even begun to understand what faith in God meant. For the first time he turned his eyes away from the hell he feared and looked upward.

So, instead of stepping up to the women and showing off his piety, he approached them humbly, and confessed that his heart was full of doubt and trouble. Could they show him what it was that made them so glad?

"Oh," answered one of them, "we are only poor ignorant women who don't know how to explain things properly. You must come and talk to our minister, the good Mr. John Gifford. He is a real man of God and he will help you. To get to his house you must go across the bridge, straight on past St. Mary's church and over the cross roads till you come to St. John's. Mr. Gifford lives at the Hospital"—that was a kind of almshouse—"under the great archway. If he is at home he will gladly talk to you."

"This Mr. Gifford," asked Bunyan, "is he a Church of England minister?"

"No," he was told, "he is an Independent. We belong to his church not because we are in the parish of St. John, but because we are all believers in that way of worship. People cannot become members unless the church meeting agrees that they are really sincere, good-living Christians."

*　　*　　*

So on Sunday Bunyan made his way into Bedford, over the river, and quietly took his place at the back of St. John's church to hear John Gifford preach. He liked the sermon; he liked especially the man who preached it. He felt sure that he truly believed, that he lived what he believed, and that he had found joy and peace in his believing. He liked the look of the congregation, too, work-worn people most of them, humble, gentle and sincere. Would he ever be worthy to join them? He saw the women with whom he had talked smiling at him encouragingly.

After the service he plucked up courage to ask John Gifford if he might have a talk with him; and presently he found himself sitting in the old parlour of the Hospital, looking out through the windows into the churchyard, and wondering how to begin.

I wish we knew what John Gifford looked like! But we have no portrait of him, and no writing to tell us. He must have been between forty and fifty, and one pictures him keen-faced and eagle-eyed, for he had been a soldier and an officer. He will have worn a dark coat and knee-breeches, black or dark grey, with snowy turned-down collar and hair falling away from a broad brow. John Bunyan, the uneducated tinker, felt shy.

"You are a good man, sir," he blurted out. " 'Holy Mr. Gifford' they call you. I have been a bad man—I still am—I doubt if you can help anyone who has such wicked thoughts as mine."

"Why," said John Gifford cheerily, "don't you know that I was known in Bedford for as wicked a man as ever walked its streets? But I was saved from my sins by the Lord Jesus Christ, who is able to save anyone who trusts Him. If any-one can understand your trouble, I can. Let me tell you my story.

"I come from Kent, and when the late war broke out I fought for King Charles, in fact I was a major in his army. You are younger than I, but I dare say you remember how, after the king was taken prisoner and the Royalist cause seemed lost, there was a last desperate rising in Kent?"

"I heard of it. There was a great battle at Maidstone, wasn't there, when the Parliament's General, Lord Fairfax, utterly routed the Malignants—I beg your pardon, sir, that was what we always called you! You see I was a soldier too, though on the other side. Not that it was any of my choosing, for I was swept up into the levy under Sir Samuel Luke at the age of sixteen." The "levy" was a kind of conscription.

"Ah well, that is all over, thank God, and the only king I serve now is King Jesus," went on Gifford. "However, in that battle I was taken prisoner, and condemned to be hanged. Now see how wonderfully the Lord delivered me, though I did not know Him at the time, because He wanted me for His own and had a work for me to do!

"The night before I was to be hanged, my dear sister came to say farewell to me in the gaol—and behold, she found the guards at the door asleep! My fellow-prisoners had been drinking heavily, and had fallen into a drunken stupor; only I was awake, for I wanted to be in my proper wits when my sister came. So she told me, 'Now is your chance to escape! Creep out softly, get away as fast as you can, and find some hiding

place!' So, like St. Peter—but far less worthy—
I stole out between the sleeping guards into the
dark. For three days I lay hidden in a ditch, and
when the search for me had died down I made my
way to London, where I had friends. Finally I
came to Bedford, where no one knew who I was
or what I had been. Having had some training in
medicine before the war, I set up as a doctor.

"But I was not grateful to the Lord for my
escape. I put it all down to luck and my own clever-
ness. A poor doctor I must have been, for I
spent most of my time drinking, gambling and
swearing! Any money I earned I always lost by
betting, so I grew poorer and poorer, until at last I
was ready to curse God and die. Think of that,
young man, when you are tempted to despair! But
the Scripture says, you know, that 'God desireth
not the death of a sinner', and the Lord Jesus has
likened God to a father who longs for the return of
his wandering, sinning son. One day there came
into my hands, as it were by chance—but I am sure
it was God's doing—a book written by a good man,
which somehow spoke to my soul. It brought me
up short in my wicked ways, and made me look
at myself and consider how sinful and ungrateful
I had been. When I realized this I was in despair
of ever being saved."

"Oh sir," Bunyan broke in, "that is just how I
feel!"

"But then I found the loving words of the Lord

Jesus—how He came to seek and to save that which was lost. I began to attend the meetings of these dear folk here, and though at first they could not believe that the drunken doctor was a changed man, at last they accepted me. When I had found Christ, I longed to tell others what He had done for me. I could not help speaking out, and so I found that I could preach, and God used me to help other sinners like myself. This year I was chosen by the congregation to be their minister. So now, John Bunyan, you see before you a man who was as vile a sinner as anybody, but whom the good Lord has cleansed and taken for His own. So speak up, and don't be afraid that I shall not understand!"

5

THE VALLEY OF THE SHADOW

BUNYAN moved with his family to Bedford. Partly this was so that he might more easily attend the services of St. John's, and have more fellowship with the members and more talk with John Gifford; partly because there was more work for him in the town than in Elstow village. He was coming up out of his Slough of Despond. With the help of Gifford and the kindly fellowship of the church members, he was learning to turn his face away from his own sins and shortcomings, and to trust in Jesus. He had times of glorious happiness as he grew to know his Lord better, and the dark times grew less and less.

It was just as well that this was so, for now he entered the dark valley of the Shadow of Death.

He was a very sick man. He had a cough which would not leave him, and he grew so thin that his clothes hung on his big frame like garments on a scarecrow. His friends shook their heads.

"Poor brother Bunyan is going into a consumption," they said to one another. "It looks as if he isn't long for this world. Whatever will

Mistress Bunyan do, poor thing, with three little children, and the eldest of them blind!" For Mary, Bunyan's eldest and his darling, had been blind from birth. Often he would take her in his arms and wonder what would happen to her if, as seemed very likely, he were taken away.

But Bunyan did not die. Whether it was the kindly help of his good neighbours, or his own greater peace of mind, or the prayers of the congregation—probably it was all three—he turned the corner and began to get better; and then the next blow fell. It was his dear wife who died, and left him with not three but four young children— Mary, Elizabeth, John and baby Thomas. How in the world was he to care for them?

"There's naught else to do, Brother Bunyan," a neighbourly woman told him, "but for you to marry again. These babes of yours must have a woman to look after them."

"True enough, sister," answered the sad young widower. "But who would want to marry a poor tinker and take over his four little ones—the youngest an infant, and the eldest blind?"

"I could give you a hint," smiled his friend. "There's a young wench who was a great friend of your dear wife's, and by the way I've seen her look at you I fancy——"

Bunyan knew at once whom she meant. Elizabeth—the same name as his second daughter— was very young, but a fine, capable, motherly lass

who seemed older than her years. Bunyan remembered how good she had been with the children
in those last sad hours. Would she? Ought he to
ask her?

"You just give her the chance," advised his old
friend. "She can say no fast enough, if the Lord
doesn't incline her heart that way."

However, Elizabeth had a great admiration for
John Bunyan, and a great love and pity for the
motherless children; so as soon as was proper
Bunyan married her, and they grew to love each
other dearly. As for the children, their young
stepmother was all that a mother could be.

*   *   *

Then came the third sorrow. John Gifford,
Bunyan's beloved friend and minister, fell ill and
died, not quite five years after becoming pastor of
the Bedford church. This was a grief shared by all
the congregation, who treasured up and read again
and again the beautiful letter that he wrote
to them when he knew that his Master was calling
him home. A new minister was chosen, but he did
not live long, and before he died was often ill. So
a great deal of work had to be shouldered by the
elders—deacons we should call them now—of the
Bedford church. It must have been about this
time that Bunyan began to preach.

He was much too modest to have opened his

mouth without being asked! But many of his friends had noticed how, in their private talks, he was always helpful and wise, and having come through so much sorrow and difficulty himself, was able to understand and sympathize. So at one of their gatherings someone suggested that Brother Bunyan should speak to them out of his experience of God's love. Bunyan rose up, trembling a little; but when he began to speak his heart was so filled with a burning love of God and of his friends that the words came pouring out, and the people sat silent and spell-bound. After that he was often asked to preach, sometimes in St. John's church, more often at little gatherings in the surrounding villages. When it was known that Brother Bunyan was to preach, people flocked from near and far to hear him.

Then Cromwell, the great Protector, died. There was no one strong enough to take his place, and in 1660 King Charles II was invited home. He very soon broke his promise to allow freedom of worship in Britain. The Independent congregation was turned out of St. John's, an Anglican priest was installed there, and everyone was ordered to worship according to the Book of Common Prayer. Which brings us to that November day when Bunyan was arrested and thrown into prison, there to await the coming of the judges to Bedford, and his trial.

6

"GENTLEMEN OF THE JURY, YOU SEE THIS MAN!"

"THAT John Bunyan, labourer, hath devilishly and perniciously abstained from coming to church to hear divine service, and is a common upholder of several unlawful meetings and conventicles, to the great disturbance and distraction of the good subjects of this Kingdom, contrary to the laws of our sovereign lord King Charles II."

The little court house, that once had been a chapel, was quite packed, and the air was anything but fresh. The judges held little nosegays of scented flowers, which now and again they sniffed. This was supposed to preserve them against the gaol-fever, which prisoners so often brought with them from the dirty, crowded gaols. Everyone stared at the man accused of such dreadful behaviour, who stood there so quietly. After three months in prison much of the country tan was gone from John Bunyan's skin, but his eye was bright and his face as calm as ever.

"Great disturbance and distraction, indeed!" muttered one of the townsfolk. "As quiet a man

as ever lived—a good honest craftsman too.
We've been the worse without John Bunyan to
mend our pots for us."

"Best hold your tongue, neighbour," advised
his companion. "Times are changed, and you
might find yourself where he is if you're not careful."

"Poor soul, how pale he is!" sympathized a
woman. "No wonder, after that stinking gaol."

"Not *all* the time," whispered another woman
cautiously. "He's been let out more than once to
visit his wife and children, and I know for sure
that he was at a prayer meeting in John Fenn the
hatter's house. The gaoler has come to be a friend
of his."

"Sh! Don't let anybody hear you! Listen,
the clerk's speaking to him."

*   *   *

"Well, John Bunyan," said the clerk of the
Sessions, "what do you say to this?"

"As to the first part of the charge," Bunyan
answered, "I do go to church regularly. I am a
member of the people of whom Christ is the
Head."

Judge Keelin interrupted. "But do you go to
church?" he said impatiently. "You know what I
mean—to the parish church?"

"No, I do not," said Bunyan.

"Why don't you?" the judge demanded.

"I do not find it commanded in the Word of God that I should go to the parish church."

"The Word of God commands us to pray," the judge took him up sharply.

"Indeed yes," was Bunyan's answer, "but not by the Prayer Book."

"How then do you think we ought to pray?" Judge Keelin hoped to catch out this ignorant tinker in some foolish answer, but he could hardly quarrel with Bunyan's reply.

"We are to pray with the Spirit, as the Apostle Paul said."

"Well, you can pray with the Spirit *and* with the Prayer Book," said Keelin.

"But," Bunyan explained, "the prayers in the Prayer Book were made by men; they are not the movement of the Holy Spirit within our hearts. The Apostle said, 'I will pray with the Spirit and with understanding,' not 'with the Spirit and the Prayer Book'."

There was a faint titter in the court at this answer. The judge scowled.

"What do you think prayer is?" he said roughly. "Is it to say a few words over before the people?"

"No, no!" Bunyan protested. "Men may use very fine words, and yet not pray at all. When a man really prays he is pouring out his heart before God through Christ, though perhaps his words may not be so many or so fine."

The judges, in spite of themselves, had to confess that this was true.

"And it can be done without the Prayer Book," Bunyan added.

"But," said Judge Keelin, coming back to the charge, "you must admit that it is lawful to use a form of prayer. Did not the Lord teach His disciples the Lord's Prayer? And cannot one man teach another to pray? And if so, is it not a good thing to have good prayers, made by good men, read over in church?"

Now this was truth, but not all the truth. The words of St. Paul came again into Bunyan's mind, and he answered, " 'The Spirit helpeth our weaknesses; for we know not how to pray as we ought, but the Spirit maketh intercession for us, with sighs and groanings which cannot be uttered.' The Spirit, not the Prayer Book. And besides, it is very easy to say, 'Our Father' with the mouth— but not many can truly say the first two words of that prayer, having really become the sons of God."

Once again, Judge Keelin was forced to say, "That's true."

*   *   *

The court was very quiet now. Even the judges were plainly surprised and impressed at the clear way in which this "ignorant tinker" was able to express his thoughts, and by his plain sincerity. Seeing this, Bunyan went on, speaking, eagerly, to explain what he felt of the work of the Holy Spirit. But soon the judges became bored and impatient. One cannot entirely blame them, for they must have had many other cases to try.

"But see here," said Judge Keelin. "What *have* you got against the Prayer Book?"

"First of all," Bunyan began, "it is not commanded in the Word of God, so we do not feel bound to use it if we do not need it."

"You don't find it commanded in the Word of God that you shall go to Elstow, or to Bedford," sneered one of the other judges, "but you go there if you want to."

"God's Word commands me to follow my calling diligently," Bunyan answered smartly, "so if my business calls me to Elstow or Bedford or elsewhere, I am doing according to God's Word."

"Look here, this fellow is too sharp," complained another judge. "Better shut him up."

"Oh," said Judge Keelin loftily, "he can't do us any harm. We know that the Prayer Book has been used ever since the time of the Apostles."

"Show me the place in the Epistles where the Prayer Book is written," cried Bunyan, "or one text of Scripture which commands me to use it, and I will use it!" Then he paused, feeling that perhaps his quick temper was leading him to behave a little un-Christianly. He continued more gently, "But

I should not wish to forbid those who want to use the Prayer Book to keep it. For our parts, we can pray to God without it, blessed be His Name."

By this time the judges, feeling that they were getting the worst of the argument, were beginning to lose their tempers very thoroughly.

"Who's your God—Beelzebub?" shouted one.

"He's raving mad!" sneered another.

"Possessed of the devil, rather!" snapped a third.

"Enough of all this, fellow! Stop your canting," ordered Judge Keelin.

"Sir," said Bunyan, "we are commanded to exhort one another daily——"

"Who gave you authority to preach, you ranting hypocritical tinker?" thundered Keelin.

"St. Peter," answered Bunyan promptly, and gave him the text he had before quoted to Foster. But Keelin was a sharper man at argument.

"You don't properly understand the text," he said. "St. Peter said, 'As every man has a gift', and so forth. He meant, as every man has a trade, let him follow it. Now you have a gift of tinkering. You stick to that."

Bunyan could not let that pass, but Keelin was in no mood to let him expound any further.

"If you must preach, do it to your family, but not to other people," he interrupted.

"Well," said Bunyan with a smile, "if it is right

to do good to some, surely it must be better to do good to more people."

"Well," said the judge, thoroughly exasperated, "we can't waste time on you any longer. I'm not a clergyman, to go into all these arguments about Scripture. Come to the point. You confess to what you are accused of, don't you?"

"I admit that we have had many meetings together, where we have had the sweet comforting presence of the Lord among us," said Bunyan. "But I am certainly not guilty of any disturbance."

"Then," said Keelin, "hear your sentence. You must be had back to prison again, and there lie for three months; and at the end of that time, if you do not agree to go to divine service in the parish church, and leave off preaching, you must be banished. And if you are found in this country after the day you are appointed to be gone, or if you come back without a special pardon from the king, I tell you plainly, you will be hanged!"

"And I say to you," Bunyan declared boldly, "that if I was out of prison to-day, by the Grace of God I would preach the Gospel to-morrow!"

The gaoler, Bunyan's friend, plucked at his sleeve. "Come away, come away for Heaven's sake!" he muttered, "before you make their worships so angry that they have you hanged out of hand!"

So back to prison went John Bunyan.

7

"I HAVE A KEY IN MY BOSOM, CALLED PROMISE"

BEFORE his judges, Bunyan had been bold and cheerful; but that night, alone in the little room on the upper floor of the gaol, which was his cell, fear and great grief came upon him. In the darkness troubles seem far worse, and time drags heavily when one cannot sleep. He knelt on the straw mattress which was his bed and tried to pray. But at first, as happens with the best of men, distracting thoughts kept crowding into his mind. It seemed as though Heaven was empty and no comfort anywhere.

"Oh my dear wife!" he groaned, but silently, for he did not wish to wake his fellow-prisoners, whose snores he could hear through the thin walls—"Oh, my poor little children! What will become of you? My little blind Mary, what will your life be like, without your father to take care of you? You may be beaten, you may have to beg in the streets, you may suffer cold, hunger, nakedness and a thousand calamities, though I cannot bear to think that the wind should blow upon you! I am like a man who is pulling down his house on the heads of his wife and children! And yet, I must do it, I *must* do it."

Softly at last the answer stole into his heart, in the words of the Bible that he knew so well: "Leave thy fatherless children; I will preserve them alive, and let thy widow trust in Me."

"Come," Bunyan reproved himself, "do I really imagine that God cannot look after my family unless I am there to help Him? He, who loves them even more than I do? For shame, John! Trust them to God."

But then, being only human, however brave and strong, he could not help wondering what fate was in store for himself. The judge had said that he might be banished. What would he do in a foreign land, a poor uneducated tinker, who had not a word of any language except his own? He pictured himself wandering, homeless, cold and hungry, among strangers who as like as not would treat him as an enemy, to lie down at last by the wayside and die like a stray dog in a ditch, or a poor forlorn sheep parted from the flock. But he was too sturdy and cheerful in spirit to dwell on those fancies long. He thought of the early Christians, and especially of St. Paul, wandering from one city to another and persecuted everywhere, and knew that he was one of a glorious company.

*   *   *

Then he thought of the threat that he might be hanged. He did not know then that, even in those cruel times, there was no law in England that would hang a man merely for his religious opinions. He feared that the judge's words might be true, and that he might have to die for his faith; and a great shudder shook him.

"I am not fit to die!" his soul cried out. "My mind is full of faithless thoughts. How shall I be saved while I am in this condition?" He imagined himself dragged out through the streets of Bedford, with the crowd jeering at him and throwing filth at him. He could see the gibbet, with the platform under it and the ladder which he must climb to have the rope put round his neck, the dreadful minute before the support was kicked away from under him, and he fell.

"I can never face it!" he thought. "How shamed I should be to go to my death with a pale face and legs that tremble so that I can't climb the ladder! Perhaps I shall faint with fear, and everyone will hoot at the cowardly tinker. I shall disgrace my Lord—I know I shall!"

He nearly fainted then and there with horror. And still no comfort came. That is often the way of things, that we are so tossed about with the storm of trouble that we cannot hear God's answer, though it is there at hand all the time.

But the strong mind and heart of John Bunyan were not to be overthrown. "I am here to witness for the Word and Way of God," he told himself stoutly, "and whatever the consequences I must not flinch an hair's breadth from it. God may choose whether He will comfort me now, or when I come to my death; but I have no choice, but to stand by what is right. Very well then, I am for going on, whether I have comfort now or not. I will leap off the ladder blindfold into Eternity, sink or swim, come Heaven, come hell. Lord Jesus, if Thou wilt catch me, do. If not, I will venture all for Thy Name. Not for the reward of Heaven, for I do not know if I shall ever get there; but for the sake of serving Thee, O Lord."

And with that, peace came into his heart. The prisoner fell asleep with a smile upon his lips.

8

"CHRISTIAN HAD SOME RESPITE"

"A WORD in your ear, Master Gaoler."

"Eh? What is it?" The gaoler, a decent, good-natured man, roused himself from his comfortable off-duty doze.

"As a friend of yours, I thought I'd better warn you. You are to have visitors this afternoon. I hope all your birds are in their cages."

"What's this?" The gaoler sat up, startled. "What visitors?"

"Some of the magistrates are coming to the gaol, to make sure that all the prisoners are safe; particularly the preaching tinker, John Bunyan. Someone has been telling tales of you, I reckon."

"Great heavens! I'm a ruined man!"

"What, have you let him out again? What a plague do you allow him to come and go for like a free man? Send for him—send for him!"

"I can't do that," cried the stricken gaoler.

"Why, don't you know where he is?"

"I know where he is, all right. But he's in London."

"In London! Why, what a fool you must be, to allow a prisoner so much liberty!"

"He's trustable. He always comes back. Besides, so you see, to my way of thinking he ought not to be in prison at all. He was committed for three months. Well, the three months is up, and still no order for his release, or any news of a fresh trial. And him such a good, peaceable man. You'd be surprised what a power he has over the other prisoners, common ruffians as most of them are. I've had no trouble with any of them since John Bunyan was put here."

"Still I don't see why you let him go out."

"Well, it began with one of his friends who was visiting him telling him of a poor woman in that congregation of his who was mortal sick, and in great trouble of mind, and longed to speak with him. Now I'm a good churchman myself, and no one can say otherwise, but I must say that this Bunyan has a more comforting way with him than any priest I know. So when he gave a great sigh, and said to his friend, 'I wish that I could go to her!' I couldn't help speaking up and saying, 'Well then, John, you slip off to see her—only mind and be back before nightfall.' So one thing led to another, you know. He's often out o' Sundays, and I surmise he goes to church—but mind you, I don't ask where! And this time, there was some folk in London that greatly wanted to speak to him. Besides, he'd a bit of a book he'd been writing, that he wanted to get printed——"

"What, a tinker writing a book! That's a good joke!"

"Ah, you may laugh, but he's a wonderful hand with a pen, tinker or no tinker! Sometimes I've listened when he was reading bits of his book to the friends that come to see him, and I can tell you, they pricked my heart. Well, howsoever, yesterday he rode to London, and to-morrow he's to be back. And back he will come, you may be sure, but too late. I'm like to lose my job, and lucky if I'm not whipped for my pains. As for John Bunyan, poor soul, as like as not it'll be chains on his ankles. Maybe they'll even clap him in the dungeons under the gaol." The gaoler dropped his head in his hands and groaned.

*   *   *

"Why, my good friend Master Gaoler, what's the trouble?" cried a hearty voice, and the gaoler sprang to his feet with a cry of joy.

"John Bunyan! Never was I gladder to see any man! But what brings you back, a day before your time?"

"Why, I hardly know," answered Bunyan thoughtfully. "But I had a strong feeling that I must come back, so I left my business in London and rode hard, and here I am."

"Well, upstairs and into your room as quick as possible," cried the gaoler, "and no one's to know you've ever been out of it. The magistrates are coming this afternoon, hoping to catch you away. But from this time on you can come and go as you please, for it's plain you know when to come back better than I can tell you."

However, the gaoler spoke too soon. Although this time he was not caught, Bunyan's expeditions came to be too well known. For a long time he was kept so closely confined that, as he put it, he "durst not look out of the door".

And now the time was come for the next Sessions, when a different set of judges were to come to Bedford. John Bunyan hoped that, having served his sentence, he might now be released.

9

"MY TROUBLE WAS ALWAYS SUCH, AS MADE ME KNOCK THE HARDER"

THE midsummer Sessions were just over, and the two judges, Hales and Twysden, with some of the local magistrates, sat resting themselves in a private room of the Swan Inn at Bedford. The wine was on the table, the long clay pipes were lit, and they were congratulating themselves that a troublesome business was over. So they were not best pleased when there came a knock at the door.

"Come in!"

A young woman, not much more than a girl, poorly dressed but very neat and clean, stepped inside, dropped a curtsey, and stood trembling and hesitating.

"Bless me, if it isn't Mistress Elizabeth Bunyan, wife of that fellow John Bunyan the preacher, that obstinate ranter," exclaimed Justice Hales. "What do you want now?"

"My lord," faltered Elizabeth, "I make bold to come again to your lordships to know what shall be done to my husband. He has served his three months in prison, and more, and he should have come before you again this Session, but the clerk would not put down his name."

"I told you before, when you brought me your petition in court, that I could do nothing for you," said Hales impatiently. "Your husband was lawfully convicted."

"He is kept wrongfully in prison," declared Elizabeth. "He was clapped into gaol before there was any proclamation against his meetings."

"He is a pestilent fellow," broke in Mr. Chester, one of the local justices. "Before the Sessions, we sent a Mr. Cobb to him, to argue with him and try to persuade him to promise to give up his preaching. But he was as stubborn as a mule."

"Mr. Chester"—Elizabeth turned to him indignantly—"if you hadn't interfered when I spoke to Mr. Hales here in court, I think he would have listened to me."

"I'm a Bedford man," retorted Chester, "and I know that your husband was lawfully convicted, and that he confessed."

"He was not lawfully convicted, and he did not confess to any crime!" Elizabeth lost her shyness in her anger at this injustice. "All my husband said was that he had been at several meetings, where there was preaching of the Word, and prayer, and God was with them."

"Your husband is a breaker of the peace, and

has been convicted by law," said Judge Twysden angrily.

"Fetch the Statute Book," Judge Hales told the clerk.

"He was *not* lawfully convicted," Elizabeth persisted.

"I say he *was* convicted," cried the obstinate Mr. Chester. "Here it is written down in the Statute Book."

"It is false!" Elizabeth's eyes flashed and the colour came into her face.

"But here it is, written down," repeated Chester—as if it must be true because it was written!

* * *

Elizabeth took a grip of her temper, and continued more mildly: "My lords: I went to London to see if I could get my husband's liberty, and I spoke with Lord Barkwood, one of the House of Lords. I had prepared a petition, and he took it to the House of Lords, and they considered it. But they said that *they* had not the power to do anything, he must be released by *you*, my lords, at the next Session. Now I have come to you, and you won't do anything about it!" She was nearly crying again.

The judges did not know what to say to this, so they said nothing, and pretended not to hear.

Only Mr. Chester muttered again, "It's written down, it's written down."

"Even if it is, it is not true," exclaimed the exasperated Elizabeth.

"The man's a perfect plague, the worst in the country," went on Chester.

"Look here, my good woman," Judge Twysden said, "will your husband give up preaching? If he will, we will see him."

Much as Elizabeth longed to have her husband home, she knew he would never agree to this. Boldly she spoke up. "My lords, he will never leave off preaching as long as he has breath."

"See here," exclaimed Judge Twysden, completely losing patience, "why do we waste time arguing over this fellow? He is a breaker of the peace."

"We only want to live peaceably," protested Elizabeth.

"As for this woman," Twysden went on, "she had the impudence to throw a petition into my coach as I was going to the court house."

"And you wouldn't take any notice! I had to try everything. Here is my husband who only wants to live quietly and get on with his business, so as to keep his family—and you keep him in prison. And I am left with four small children, one of them blind, and nothing to live on but the charity of our neighbours."

"What!" said Judge Hales. "Four children?

You look too young for that." He was a good-natured fellow, and had been moved by Elizabeth's courage—especially when she spoke of going to London, which was a great journey for a young, poor woman in those days.

"They are not my own," explained Elizabeth. "My husband was married before. I lost my own baby when my husband was arrested," she added sadly.

"You poor woman!" said the kindly Hales.

"Oh, don't listen to her!" cried Twysden. "She pleads her poverty just to work on our feelings. I expect her husband earns more by his running up and down preaching than by honestly working at his trade."

"What is his trade?" Hales asked, and one of the local people said that he was a tinker.

"Yes, he is a tinker, and a poor man," spoke up Elizabeth, "and so you despise him and deny him justice."

"Look, my poor woman," Judge Hales told her gently, "the only thing for you to do is to apply to the king for a pardon."

"If he gets a pardon, he'll only start preaching again," exclaimed Mr. Chester.

"How should a poor woman like myself apply to the king?" cried Elizabeth desperately.

"It would be cheaper to get a Writ of Error, stating that a mistake was made," Judge Hales went on.

"But if you won't hear my husband, what is the use of telling me that?"

"I have given you the best advice I can," said Judge Hales.

"He is a convicted man—it's written down!" cried Chester.

"That's enough of this business," declared Twysden.

*   *   *

Elizabeth saw that it was all no use. Hales meant kindly by her, but he was not a strong enough character to get his way against Twysden, who cared nothing and was bored by the whole affair; and Chester was actively against Bunyan. Sadly disappointed, she turned away, but at the door she burst into a storm of tears.

"It was not so much that they were so hard-hearted against us," she told her husband when she reported to him what had happened, "but to think what a sad account such poor creatures will have to give at the coming of the Lord, when they will have to answer for all they have done in their lives."

Bunyan was not brought to trial again, or ever properly sentenced, but left in prison for the next twelve years.

IO

"IN THOSE DAYS WE WERE AFRAID TO WALK THE STREETS"

ON a spring Sunday in April, 1670, when John Bunyan had been for nearly ten years in prison, the congregation of his friends met for worship in the house of John Fenn the hatter. They were all humble, ordinary folk—Samuel Fenn, John's brother, also a hatter; John Bardolf, a maltster; Nicholas Hawkins, a cutler; Thomas Cooper, a heelmaker; Daniel Rich, a tanner; also a baker, a blacksmith, a pipemaker and other small tradesmen. Among the women we know of Mrs. Covington, a grocer's wife, and a widow named Mrs. Tilney, who was rather better off than most of her neighbours, and much loved by them for her kindness and generosity.

The years had been hard on them all. John Fenn and Thomas Cooper were only recently released from prison, and many others had from time to time been in gaol for their beliefs. But being locked up in Bedford gaol had its bright side, for was not their beloved leader, John Bunyan, there to welcome them, as St. Paul did the Christians when he was under house arrest in Rome? John

Fenn had brought one of Bunyan's brave, en-
couraging letters to read to the meeting.

*   *   *

Indeed, they needed encouragement. A new
Conventicle Act, harsher than the first, had just
been passed, and on that bright morning the men,
women and children crowded so closely into Fenn's
back room felt as though great thunder clouds
were towering in the sky, darkening the sunlight
and threatening a heavy storm.

The storm broke towards the end of their meeting. There came the expected hammering at the
door, and the shout, "Open, in the king's name!"
Two constables pushed their way in, and while one
guarded the door (not that anyone tried to escape)
the other read in a loud, bullying voice a warrant
for the arrest of all those present.

"Come along now, all of you, to Mr. Justice
Foster's house," he shouted. "Hurry up now,
don't keep his worship waiting! Step lively!"

This Mr. Foster was the brother-in-law of the
Justice Wingate who had first arrested Bunyan;
the same Foster who had tried to trap him in talk
at Harlington Hall.

Calm and orderly the congregation passed out
into the street, though the women clung to their
husbands' arms and the children to their mothers'
skirts. Many of their neighbours, coming from the

service at the parish church, stopped to see what was happening. A few idle boys began to hoot, but it was the constables who got most of the scowls and hissing from the more respectable folk.

"It's a downright shame, so it is."

"Decent, peaceable folk, all of them."

"Honest traders and hardworking craftsmen, too, that would never cheat a neighbour."

"Poor souls, they'll be ruined. That Mr. Justice Foster has a strange hate for every Nonconformist. He'll skin 'em of everything they have."

"Ay, right bitter he is against 'em. And why? They never did him any harm."

"They do say he's never forgiven John Bunyan for getting the better of him in argument, ten years since, when the good man was first arrested."

"Well, I'm loyal to the king, God bless him, and the parish church is good enough for me. But I can't see what harm these poor creatures are doing, to want to pray in their own way."

So they muttered and murmured as the little procession passed along the narrow cobbled streets and disappeared into the handsome town house of Mr. Justice Foster.

*　　*　　*

The justice, sitting at his table with a satisfied grin on his face, was harsher even than the Act. Five shillings fine was the law for the first offence, ten shillings for the second—a big enough sum in those days for poor folk to pay. But Mr. Foster began by fining them as much as he thought he could get out of them. Naturally they had not the money with them to pay the fine at once, so he gave them a few days to collect it.

"Friday next," he told them. "See that you have your fines ready, or my men will collect your household goods to the value of them."

"How shall we ever pay it?" moaned some as they made their way home. "We shall be ruined utterly."

Friday began badly for the officers of the law. Old Thomas Battison, a churchwarden, was put in charge of the business, and he and his men marched down in fine style to the house of Bardolf the maltster. They had not gone far before they gathered another following, for out poured the sympathetic neighbours, some jeering and some scolding.

Bardolf, a good business man, was ready for them, standing before his malthouse door.

"Where's your fine, John Bardolf?"

"I haven't got so much money, and well your master knows it," replied Bardolf.

"Open up then, and let us have your malt in payment."

"Ah," said Bardolf, "but the malt isn't mine, so you can't take it. I've sold it."

"You can't take another man's malt, old Battison," shouted someone in the crowd. "That's not the law."

Battison scratched his head in perplexity. There was a yell of laughter, and as he whisked round to see who was jeering he felt something flapping at his back. Some bad boys had stolen up and pinned a calf's tail to his coat! Very red and angry, and feeling a good deal of a fool, Battison decided to leave Bardolf alone for the time being, and led his party to the grocer, Covington, whose wife had been at the meeting.

"Five shillings from you, Edward Covington, for allowing your wife to attend a conventicle."

"You just try stopping my wife from going where she's a mind to!" argued Covington. "It's no affair of mine what she does."

"Where is your wife, then?"

"Not at home."

"I'll have something out of you, at any rate," blustered Battison, and stepping into the house he seized the handsomest article there, a large brass kettle. "This will do. Here——" to one of his men—"carry this along to the Swan Inn."

"Kettle stealer! Kettle stealer!" yelled the boys in the crowd. Battison's men looked sheepish.

"Look here, master, I'm not your porter," said the man he had ordered to take the kettle. " 'Tain't my business to lug kettles about."

"Nor mine neither—nor mine—I shan't, that's

flat"—and so said all of them. At last Battison bribed a boy with sixpence to take the heavy kettle to the inn.

"Nay," proclaimed the innkeeper, straddling his gate, "you aren't going to set that down in *my* yard. I'm no receiver of stolen goods."

"And I'm not going to lug it no further, master," announced the boy, setting down the kettle and rubbing his arm. "Mortal heavy, it is, and all my mates laughing at me, too."

So there the kettle sat, in the middle of the street, and Battison went off in a fine rage to report to Mr. Foster that he had had no luck that day.

*   *   *

Foster, of course, was not to be so easily defeated. Things now took a serious turn. A file of soldiers was called up, and on Saturday Battison marched with them to Bardolf's house, broke down the doors of the malthouse and took away fourteen sacks of malt. What the real owner said about it we are not told!

Sunday morning saw the worshippers dauntlessly gathered again at John Fenn's house. They had barely started their service before Battison and his constables appeared with another warrant.

"We will obey, but not until we have finished our worship," said Fenn firmly.

Three men could not very well drag a whole

congregation away, so, fuming and baffled, Battison again sent a message to Mr. Foster.

"Tell old Battison," said Foster impatiently, "to go and get some men he can depend on and *force* the ranters to come out."

Once again names were taken and fines imposed. This time Foster wasted no days. On the Monday morning he himself, with Battison, the constables and a file of soldiers, appeared early in Bedford town, intent on doing the job thoroughly. Even so, they found many of the shops and houses empty, for the humbler members of the congregation had quietly disappeared.

"The town looked like a country village, there were so few people," wrote someone who saw it all. "And with all the shops shuttered, it reminded one of the days of the plague, when they wrote upon the doors 'The Lord have mercy on us!'"

Two families had not been able to get away, being in grievous trouble. The children of Hawkins the cutler and Honeylove the shoemaker were ill with the smallpox; a terribly common disease in those days, when there was no vaccination. However, in this case it proved a protection, for no one would go into the infected homes, and the poor people were left in peace.

The leaders of the congregation had stayed to face the music. Thomas Cooper, the heelmaker, had three cartloads of wood ready to make into heels and lasts for shoes, and Foster ordered his men to carry all this away. It was worth much more than Cooper's 40s. fine.

"I'd rather they had taken all my household goods!" Cooper lamented. "How shall I earn my living now?"

Foster seized the best coat of Rich the tanner, and emptied the shop of Spencer the grocer. From Isaac the blacksmith they took all his tools, even his anvil. Next they came to the house of Tom Arthur, the pipemaker.

Now Arthur was quite a famous pipemaker in his day, and his initials, T.A., have been found on the little clay bowls of pipes turned up from time to time by workmen digging in Bedford town. Arthur's door was locked, but he opened it at once.

"Your fine, pipemaker," said Foster curtly.

"How much is it?" Arthur asked anxiously.

"Eleven pounds."

Arthur started. "I don't remember that you put it at as much as that yesterday," he protested. "May I see the warrant? Thank you. But—but it says here only six pounds—and that's enough for a poor pipemaker to pay."

"Five pounds more for keeping your door locked," Foster snapped.

"It is not just!" cried Arthur. "I did not keep you waiting. Besides, I haven't got so much money."

"All right. If you haven't the money, we'll take the goods," replied Foster.

"But sir, if you take everything, what shall my children do? Must they starve?" said poor Arthur.

"So long as you are a rebel, your children shall starve," was the rough answer. "Constables, do your duty!"

"Indeed, I am no rebel!" pleaded the pipe-maker, but it was of no avail. Battison and the constables swept up any of his furnishings and pots and pans that took their fancy, and worse still, they gathered all the wood he had set up for firing the furnaces in which his clay pipes were baked. Some of the soldiers muttered that it was a shame to ruin the poor man in this way, but they dared not disobey Mr. "Justice" Foster.

* * *

What roused the greatest grief and anger was the treatment of Mrs. Tilney, the well-to-do widow. Foster had even less mercy on her than on the small tradesmen. Her fine was £20, and no doubt, given time, she could easily have paid it; but she had not got such a sum handy on a Monday afternoon. Foster ordered his men to take her goods.

Tables, cupboards, chairs, featherbeds, blankets, the very hangings of her room and the sheets off her bed were carried away, leaving the once comfortable house as bare as a barn. Foster took absolutely no notice of the angry cries, and sobs and sighs and complainings of the women who had gathered round their friend but could do nothing to save her. But Mrs. Tilney herself stood calmly in the midst of them with a brave smile on her face, though her heart must have bled to see the precious household treasures, given her by her dead husband, all carted off pell-mell.

"You come along with me, my dear, since the brutes have left you nothing to sleep on!"

"No, come to me, and stay as long as you like! You'll be welcome. Many's the good turn I've had from you."

"I'll not forget how you nursed me and cared for the children when I was sick. You come with me!"

So they all clamoured, but Mrs. Tilney shook her head. "No, I'd rather not sleep out of my own house," she declared. "It's about all that's left to me. If one of you good neighbours will just lend me a pair of sheets, I shall do very well."

John Fenn and his brother Samuel both lost all the hats in their shops, and many others had taken from them their means of earning. It was a hard time; but they stuck together, met for worship in little groups secretly, and helped each other as much as they could.

The letters that John Bunyan sent to them from his prison were the greatest comfort to them. Separated from them though he was, he had become their leader and, though not in name, their pastor.

II

"THEIR NAMES WERE KNOWLEDGE, EXPERIENCE, WATCHFUL, AND SINCERE"

NO persecution lasts for ever. By the end of the year 1671 Mr. Foster and his like had grown tired of harrying the Nonconformists, for all they had got from it was the scorn and dislike of the townsfolk, and a good deal of mockery too. So that, although the "conventicles" were still officially forbidden, the church members were able to gather for their meetings without being interfered with. At any rate, if we study the worn old book that holds the records of the Bedford church, we shall find a very important entry for January 21st, 1672. Here is the record just as it stands:

"After much seeking God by prayer, and sober conference formerly had, the congregation did at this meeting with joynt consent (signified by solemne lifting up of their hands) call forth and appoint our brother John Bunyan to the pastorall office or eldership. And he accepting thereof, gave up himself to serve Christ and His Church in that charge; and received of the elders the right hand of fellowship.

"The same time also, the congregation having had long experience of the faithfulness of brother John fenne in his care for the poor, did after the same manner solemnly choose him to the honourable office of deacon, and committed the poor and purse to him, and he accepted thereof, and gave himself up to ye Lord and them in that service."

There, too, we read the names of others who had proved themselves steadfast under persecution, and who were now appointed to be elders of the church.

* * *

Was John Bunyan, then, freed from his prison, that the congregation ventured to appoint him as their pastor? No, he was not yet actually freed, but he was now able to come and go to a certain extent, and what he could not do in person he did by writing, and in consultation with his friends John Fenn and the other elders. But surprising happenings were on the way.

Little did that wily, easy-going, self-indulgent king, Charles II, care for the tinkers, hatters, pipe-makers, cobblers and so forth of little towns like Bedford; no more did the great Lords of the Upper House of Parliament, or the busy politicians of the House of Commons. But what those great folk did in March, 1672, certainly made things much easier for the humble ones.

King Charles, having artfully wheedled a large sum of money out of the French king, felt himself strong enough to do without Parliament. He dissolved it, and promptly did what he had long wanted to do—he issued a Declaration of Indulgence which forbade persecution of anyone for their religious beliefs. This, of course, was because he favoured the Roman Catholics, but the Nonconformists benefited too.

Bunyan walked out of Bedford gaol, a free man at last, and at once applied for a licence to preach, which he got without any difficulty. He must have wondered if he were dreaming, and would wake up in his cell again! But really he was very wide awake, with a lot of business to attend to.

For the king's Declaration went on to say:

"That there may be no pretence of any of our subjects to continue their illegal meetings and conventicles, we do declare that we shall from time to time allow a sufficient number of places, as they shall be desired, in all parts of this our kingdom, for the use of such as do not conform to the Church of England, to meet and assemble in order to their public worship and devotion."

Bunyan and the elders at once set about finding a place where they could all meet comfortably, instead of crowding into John Fenn's back room.

Bedford town in those days was not the thickly built place it is now, but had within its walls large paddocks and orchards. One of the church members had such a field, close under the Castle Mount, with a roomy barn in it, and this was the first meeting place of what is now the Bedford Baptist Church. The present church is built on that very site!

Bunyan did not consider only his own congregation. He thought of the many other smaller congregations scattered in the neighbourhood, who would be glad of a secure meeting place not far from their homes; and he knew of a number of good honest men among them who would be willing to act as their pastors. So he drew up a list of twenty-five preachers and thirty buildings, and applied for licences for them all. They were very simple—mostly barns and private houses—and he took a loving interest in each one.

*　　*　　*

In all weathers he might be seen riding about the Bedfordshire lanes, stopping to preach at farms or village greens or the market places of small towns through which he passed. "Bishop Bunyan" people called him, half laughing and half in earnest; and indeed he was to his people a true "shepherd".

His flock were not always peaceful, obedient

sheep. Sheep seldom are, as any shepherd will tell you. They were just ordinary folk like the rest of us, and needed careful shepherding if some of them were not to go scampering off into dangerous ways. If, after being first reasoned with, either by Bunyan himself or one of his deacons, and then scolded, they persisted in their naughtiness, they were put out of membership. If this seems harsh, we must remember that it was most important that the Nonconformists should keep a good reputation; for they still had many enemies on the watch for excuses to forbid them their meetings once more.

For example, one John Rush got so shockingly drunk that he had to be carried home insensible.

A Mrs. Landy was careless about coming to services, and what was worse, she was allowing her children to become careless too. She had even taught them to play cards! Not that card-playing in itself is worse than any other game, but that it is so much connected with betting and gambling.

Then there was that naughty girl Lizzie Maxey, who got a public scolding for calling her father a liar and being rude to her mother; and Lizzie Burntwood, who was a saucy little flirt. Let us hope these two young girls mended their ways.

Nehemiah Cox, on the other hand, was one of the deacons elected when Bunyan became pastor. He was exactly some people's idea of a Puritan, a narrow-minded man who behaved himself very precisely, but he had one of the worst faults a church member can have—he was a mean-minded gossip and a tale-bearer. That was the sort of thing great-hearted Bunyan could not stand, and when he had finished with him Nehemiah was a shamed and sorry man, and promised faithfully to be more generous in future.

All these cases, and many more, are set down in the church records, so that we come to feel that we know these men and women as they go about their business in the narrow Bedford streets under the overhanging gables, or in the fields of the pleasant countryside. It was on the whole a peaceful and a happy time after the storm.

12

THE PILGRIM'S PROGRESS

THREE years after his release, Bunyan was in prison again—not, this time, in the town gaol, but in a small building on the bridge that crossed the River Ouse. A few years before, a great flood had swept this prison away, but it had just been rebuilt. Those who gave the order for its repair could not know that something was to happen there which would become known all over the world!

"Put not your trust in princes," says the Bible. Bunyan never did that. He knew very well that when King Charles made his Declaration of Indulgence without the consent of Parliament he was acting illegally, and when Parliament met again the Indulgence would certainly be revoked. That was what happened. Bunyan lost his preaching licence, but of course he went on preaching. That was how he came to be in the little prison on the bridge.

During his long imprisonment before, he had done a great deal of writing—books and pamphlets as well as letters. During the last three years he had been too busy with his pastorate to write much, but now he made the most of his forced rest, and settled down to write a book which he called *The Strait Gate: the Way and Race of Saints*. It was while he was occupied with this that his imagination suddenly lit up. He seemed actually to see his "saints"—by which he did not mean extremely good people, but, like St. Paul, just ordinary men and women trying to live the Christian life. There was his poor Christian, burdened by his sins, looking for the Gate and falling into the Slough of Despond. Bunyan knew just how clinging and sticky this would be, for was there not a swamp in a field below his old cottage at Elstow, into which he had several times fallen as a boy? The story began to grow, picture after picture, conversation after conversation, all sorts of people walking into it, until he longed for nothing better than to sit down and write it all out just as it came to him. But he pulled himself up.

"This won't do, John!" he told himself severely. "I must put all these fancies away for the time being, and get on with the book I am writing."

So he resolutely finished *The Strait Gate* and sent it out to be printed. Now, he could really enjoy himself! Never had he been so happy in any of his writing. The ideas flowed out faster than he could get them down. Day after day at the rough table his quill scratched away, and the gaoler peering in, or his friends visiting him, would see only the broad shoulders bent above his work, the thick curly hair, now streaked with grey, falling over an absorbed face that was now stern and grave, now alight with fun, now flushed and excited as he described a stirring battle such as Christian's fight with Apollyon.

He brought his Pilgrim in at the Gate, through the Interpreter's House, up the Hill Difficulty and into the Palace Beautiful; then, slipping and sliding, down into the Valley of Humiliation and the awful Shadow of Death. How well Bunyan knew that route! He knew, too, Vanity Fair. Perhaps on one of his visits to London he had seen the great Fair of St. Bartholomew, just such a noisy, rumbustious, rackety place! By-path Meadow and the Castle of Giant Despair—had Bunyan in his travels ever been deceived by just such a pleasant footpath, that looked like an easy short cut and led him astray? And so up to the Delectable Mountains.

He knew all the people whom Christian met with on the way. Good Evangelist—was that his friend Mr. Gifford? Noble Faithful, buoyant Hopeful, the wise, kindly dwellers in the Palace Beautiful; and the Shepherds—were they perhaps his fellow workers, the elders of the congregation? And on the other side vain Talkative, brisk Ignorance, pompous Mr. Worldly Wiseman, the malignant jury in Vanity Fair—certainly he had met them all. As we read, we seem to know them too, though they do use a different kind of speech from ours.

*   *   *

When Bunyan had got as far as the Delectable Mountains, there was an interruption. He was set free! By now he was a well-known man with many influential friends, and some of these had been working on his behalf. So back he went to his congregation and his care for them. But *The Pilgrim's Progress* had taken such a hold of him that he could not let it alone. He finished off, and then wondered what to do about it.

It was not in the least like anything he had written before. Would anyone else like it? Would it be at all helpful to them? He read it first to his wife and family. There were five children now—blind Mary had died (Bunyan missed her sorely, but rejoiced to think that now she was safe); John was a young man working at his father's trade, Elizabeth in her late teens, and Thomas a big boy; and there were the two little ones born to his second wife, Sarah and Joseph. Of course they all loved the Pilgrim, and clamoured to have the book printed.

Next, Bunyan tried it out on some of his congregation. Here he found varying opinions.

"Some said, John, print it; others said, Not so.

Some said it might do good, others said, No."

Thus Bunyan wrote in the rhyming preface to the book. There were some, too, who thought that he wrote in altogether too homely a style, using just the sort of talk that people spoke in the streets of Bedford. Others objected that it was even funny in parts, as where Christian and Pliable flounder about·in the Slough of Despond, or in the bragging speeches of Mr. Talkative. Bunyan was no sour-faced kill-joy. He loved a good laugh in the right place.

"Now was I in a strait; and did not see
    What was the best thing to be done by me:
    At last I thought, Since you are thus divided
    I print it will; and so the case decided."

It was a tremendous success at once. The first edition was sold out, and a second, and a third, all in one year. It was read by all manner of people, whether they were Nonconformists or not. The name of John Bunyan became famous. It may be supposed that enough money came from it to make the little house in Bedford more comfortable, and for Bunyan to be able to give up his tinkering altogether.

Encouraged by this, Bunyan, having told the story of a good man battling his way through dangers and difficulties to the Celestial City, now decided to write the life of a Mr. Badman, sliding downhill from small sins to greater ones, committing every kind of evil. But though the book is cleverly written, somehow it was not a success. People in those days (whatever they may do now) did not care to read about a man who was bad all through; and very likely Bunyan himself did not enjoy writing it. Something much better was taking shape in his mind.

Naturally his children were always asking him, "But what happened to Christian's wife? And didn't you say that he had some little children? Surely you aren't going to leave them in the City of Destruction!"

And his wife Elizabeth, with a little toss of her head, would say, "I don't see why women shouldn't go on pilgrimage to the Celestial City."

"Women can't wear armour and fight battles," argued one of the boys.

"Women have as great hearts as men," answered his mother, and John Bunyan smote his knee.

"You have hit it, wife! We will send all the family on pilgrimage, and we will give them the warrior Great-heart to be their champion."

*   *   *

Thus Bunyan settled down to write the second part of *The Pilgrim's Progress*. Although it has some exciting fights in it, it is a much gentler

book than the first part. It is interesting to
notice that in his journey Christian met, on
the whole, more bad people than good: but
as Christiana and her children, and their dear
little friend Mercy, travelled on, there gathered to
them a company of thoroughly fine men and
women. Sturdy old Honest, brave Mr. Valiant-for-
Truth, resolute Mr. Standfast, Mr. Ready-to-
Halt the dauntless cripple and his friend Mr.
Feeble-Mind, and poor Mr. Despondency and
Much-Afraid, his daughter, who would not let
their nervous fears overcome them.

There are besides so many homely incidents,
such as the boys eating stolen fruit and falling sick,
little James sick with fear in the Valley of the
Shadow, Mercy sewing garments for the poor;
and all of them sitting down with good appetites
to the meals provided in the houses where they
rest by the way. One may venture to guess
that Mrs. Bunyan and the girls had quite a lot to
do with the writing of the second part of *The
Pilgrim's Progress*!

13

"MR. VALIANT-FOR-TRUTH WAS TAKEN WITH A SUMMONS"

"MR. Bunyan, I've come to ask you a favour." The young man was pale, stammering, and evidently very much upset.

"What can I do for you, my young brother?"

"You'll have heard, I'm sure, that I—that I and my father have quarrelled——"

"I know. I was very sorry to hear it. Your father lives at Reading, does he not?"

"At Reading—yes. Perhaps if we had lived nearer one another it would have been easier to make it up. Mr. Bunyan, I know it was mostly my fault, and I want to let my father know how sorry I am. But he won't agree to see me."

"How do you know that?"

"A friend who has just come from Reading tells me that my father has been brooding over the quarrel, and getting more and more angry. Now he threatens to cut me out of his will."

"Are you sure," said Bunyan shrewdly, "that it isn't the fear of losing the money that makes you want to make up the quarrel?"

The young man grew rather red. "I'll be honest

with you, sir. I confess I was troubled by it, for I'm lately married, you know, and have a young family to look after. But truly it isn't only that. My father is getting old—how if he should die, and we were still enemies? I really do long to tell him that I was in the wrong. I was wondering— sir, my father has a great respect for you. Do you think you could go and see him, and persuade him to let me come to him?"

"Well, well, I have to go to London shortly, and I will go round by Reading and try what I can do."

"God bless you, sir! I'm sure you will succeed."

*　　*　　*

"John!" protested Elizabeth after the visitor had gone, "why need you go to Reading yourself? It is miles out of your way, and you know you haven't been well since that bad attack of the sweating sickness last year. Why don't you write a letter?"

"It wouldn't be the same thing, my dear. The old man is obstinate—it will take a great deal of persuasion to bring him round—not to speak of love and prayer. I can't put that in a letter. I must go myself. 'Blessed are the peacemakers', you know."

Elizabeth said no more, for she knew it was of no use. But her pleasant face was lined with worry as she watched her husband ride away to the west on a bright August morning. Bunyan was only sixty, but he looked older. The long years in prison, the everlasting uncertainty of his life, the hard work, and especially the taking into his own great heart all the troubles and problems of his flock, had worn him out before his time.

So, jogging along the dusty roads on his sober nag, Bunyan came to Reading. What he said to the angry old man no one knows, but he won his victory. Very likely the father longed to be reconciled to his son, but his pride would not let him give in until the honoured Bunyan interceded. At all events, Bunyan set out for London with a rejoicing heart. He had a lot of business to attend to. In his saddlebag was the manuscript of his latest book, which he was taking to the printers. He had promised to preach several times, and there were many London friends he had to see.

Now, as so often happens in an English summer, the weather changed. Cold winds and driving rain came on, and as Bunyan rode with bent head, the water dripping from his broad hat and his cloak pulled close about him, he was soon drenched through and shivering with the cold. It was a tired, coughing old man who arrived at last at the house of John Strudwick, the friend with whom he was to stay.

"John, old friend, you must keep your bed until that cough leaves you!" Strudwick exclaimed.

"I shall be better in the morning," said Bunyan hopefully. And next day he insisted on getting up and taking the service as he had promised. One who was in the congregation and took notes said that he had never preached more lovingly. The day after he took his book to the printers, and met and talked with various people. When the first proofs of the book were ready, he must go through them to see that there were no mistakes in the meaning. As for spelling mistakes, they had to take their chance. To the end of his days Bunyan's spelling was so wild that he sometimes spelled the same word in three or four different ways!

His cough got worse instead of better. His head ached, he felt sick and dizzy; sometimes he was burning hot, sometimes trembling with chill.

"My dear John, you really must go to bed," his friend urged. "Come along—my wife has aired the sheets with a warming pan, she will make you a hot posset, and we will get the apothecary to come and prescribe a draught for you. You have a fever, I can see."

"Very well," sighed Bunyan, giving. in at last. "But I am sorry to put you and your good wife to all this trouble."

All the hot possets, all the medicine that was known at that time, could not do anything for Bunyan now. Soon he realized that he had received his summons to go over the river.

"I'll be glad to go," he told Strudwick, drawing his breath painfully. "Thank God, my affairs are all in order, and my dear wife will have enough to live on. Sarah and Joseph are old enough to be left, and the others are grown now. I shall see my little Mary, my darling—and she will see me! Best of all, I shall be with my Lord. Lord Jesus, receive my soul!"

So John Bunyan entered the Celestial City of which he had dreamed—and no doubt he found it far more wonderful and beautiful than all his imaginings.

*　　*　　*

The Pilgrim's Progress has been translated into many languages, and wherever it goes it is loved. Christians of many races, black and brown and yellow, find that it tells of their own struggles just as clearly as it does of ours. African schoolboys have acted it, Chinese artists have drawn pictures of a Chinese Christian in old-fashioned armour fighting with a Chinese Apollyon. Bunyan's Pilgrim's Hymn, "Who would true Valour see," is sung in many churches:

> "There's no discouragement
> Shall make him once relent
> His first avowed intent
> To be a pilgrim."

And do we not all know the song of the Shepherd Boy:

> "He that is down need fear no fall,
> He that is low, no pride;
> He that is humble ever shall
> Have God to be his Guide."

That was the way of John Bunyan.